ANIMALS IN DISGUISE

MICHAEL BRIGHT

WAYLAND
www.waylandbooks.co.uk

First published in Great Britain in 2020 by Wayland
Text copyright © Hodder and Stoughton, 2020

Editor: Elise Short
Designer: Lisa Peacock
Cover design: Jason Anscomb
Production controller: Inka Roszkowska
Picture research: Rachelle Morris and Diana Morris

Picture credits:
All Images Nature Picture Library as follow:
Into Arndt: 21c; Javier Aznar: 77t; Franco Banfi: 3cl, 25tr, 39t, 66, 91bl; Fred Bavendan: 62,65t, 91cla; Stephen Belcher: 33c; Emanuele Biggi: 5b, 76, 92tr; Peter Cairns: 37t; Philippe Clément: 18-19c, 88bl; Sue Daly: 4b; Georgette Douwma: 70, 71, 91br; Eric Dragesco: 14, 88cl; Michael Durham: 49t; Hanne & Jens Eriksen: 31; Suzi Eszterhas: 6c; Yukihiro Fukuda: 40-41, 50, 90cr; Nick Garbutt: front cover bcl, 43t, 44, 53t, 90tr; Edwin Giesbers: 52, 90bl; Jen Guyton: 47t, 87; Mark Hamblin: 3tl, 8, 9tr, 12, 13t, 88tr; Wim van der Heever: front cover bcr, 27c; Alex Hyde: front cover bl, 3cr, 72, 73tr, 78, 79t, 81t, 82, 83t,86, 92cla, 92cl, 92br; Donald M Jones: 17t; Michael D Kern: 45; David Kjaer: 28, 89tr; Tim Laman: 7t; Jiri Lochman: 23c; Hougaard Malan:19t; Valery Maleev: 15c; Thomas Marent : 80, 85t, 89tl, 92cr; Chris Mattison: front cover br, 48, 90cra; Diane McAllister: 11tr; Alex Mustard: front cover main,1 3tr,56-57, 60, 61, 63t, 67, 69t; 91t; Nature Production: 3bl, 41t, 51;Thomas Parent: 26; Doug Perrine: 58,91tl; Constantinos Petrinos: 5t; Linda Pitkin: 59t; Michel Poinsihnon: 36, 89bl; Roger Powell: 7b; Premaphotos: 90cl, 46; Pressephotos: 46; Thomas Rabeil: 4c, Tui de Roy: 54, 55t, 90br; Andy Sands: back cover, 74, 91tl; George Sanker: 16, 88cr; Scotland:The Big Picture: 24-25, 38, 89br; Roland Seite: 20, 64, 88bc, 91cl; Anup Shah: 10, 88tl; Brent Stephenson: 32, 89cl; Enrique Lopez-Tapia: 42, 90tl; Markus Varevuo: 30, 34, 35t, 89cr, 89crb; Dave Watts: 22, 88br; Mike Wilkes: 84, 92bl; Rod Williams: 75t; Norbert Wu: 68, 91cr; Tony Wu: 6b.

All other illustration and design elements: Shutterstock.

HB ISBN: 978 1 5263 1214 3
PB ISBN: 978 1 5263 1215 0

Printed and bound in Dubai

Wayland, an imprint of
Hachette Children's Group
Part of Hodder and Stoughton
Carmelite House
50 Victoria Embankment
London EC4Y 0DZ
An Hachette UK Company
www.hachette.co.uk
www.hachettechildrens.co.uk

The website addresses (URLs) included in this book were valid at the time of going to press. However, it is possible that contents or addresses may have changed since the publication of this book. No responsibility for any such changes can be accepted by either the author or the Publisher.

CONTENTS

SURVIVAL SKILLS

Animals have many adaptations to help them survive. Camouflage, an animals ability to blend in with its environment, is one. Animals living in deserts, where sand and light brown colours dominate, will have very different camouflage from those living in tropical rainforests, where green leaves are more common. Even more distinct are the animals in the sea. Colours actually disappear the deeper you go, until you reach the deep sea, where there is hardly any colour, because it's permanently dark! Yet, even here fish and squid use camouflage.

Low profile

There are many different ways in which animals can blend in with their background. A general buff (yellow-brown) colour of fur or feathers, like that of sand cats (see right), gives a measure of disguise in dry grasslands and deserts. Spots or stripes break up outlines in dappled woodland or dense jungle. And, a black band across the eyes effectively hides the eyes, which are normally easy to spot because of their distinctive shape.

Changing background

An animal's habitat might change with the seasons, and so too does its camouflage. Mountain hares (see pages 12–13), for example, are white in winter and mottled brown in summer. Other animals are able to match their background almost instantly. Many flatfish (see left) have pigment cells in their skin that can be changed to match a background of sand one minute and of pebbles the next.

Disappearing in the sea

In the open ocean, fish are dark on their back and light on their belly. Seen from above, the dark colour of a great white shark's back (right) matches the darkness of the sea. Seen from below, its pale underside blends in with the glow of the sunlight above. In the 'midnight zone' of the deep sea, animals go even further. Fish and squid have rows of glowing lights on their bellies that help them blend in with the very dim light from the distant surface above.

Part of the scenery

Some creatures pretend to be inanimate objects, such as sticks, leaves, flowers, tree bark, moss and lichens. In the sea, they might resemble corals, seaweeds or rocks. The strangest animals must be those that look like bird droppings, such as this bird-dropping spider (below)!

PREDATORS AND PREY

Animals use camouflage to help them catch a meal or to avoid being eaten. There are those animals that eat other animals – the predators – and those that generally eat plants, but want to stay off the menu – the prey. Predators do not want to be seen before they strike, and prey animals want to disappear from view, to avoid getting caught. Both predators and prey try to stay one step ahead of the other.

Stalkers and chasers

Predators have many different ways to catch a meal. Some predators stalk their prey. They need camouflage to be able to creep up on their target and get as close as possible before they pounce. Tigers (see left) and leopards like to pounce, but they cannot do this unless they are really close. Lions and cheetahs tend to stalk their prey and then chase it. They also need to get close, so their pursuit is as short as possible before they become exhausted.

Sit-and-wait

Ambush predators such as the Japanese angelshark (right) need to blend in with their background so unwary animals fail to see them waiting to attack. It is an energy-efficient way to hunt, as the predator does not need to run after its prey. On the downside, it has to wait patiently for something to come along, so there could be long gaps between meals. If the prey spots the predator at the last moment, however, it is usually too late. Gulp and the prey has gone!

Avoid being caught

The best strategy for prey animals is to have fur, feathers or skin matching their background, and then to keep very, very still. If they move, the illusion is broken and they are suddenly in full view. They have to move at some points in their life, however, in order to find food. If they are spotted, their only other option is to flee as fast as they can. The flying dragon lizard's first line of defence is to look like tree bark (see left), but if that fails it escapes by gliding to another tree.

Looking after young

Young animals, especially those growing up in open countryside, are especially vulnerable to predators, and different species have different ways to protect their offspring. Birds' eggs may be disguised as pebbles, for example, and chicks like these stone curlew chicks (right), can be so beautifully camouflaged against the ground that they are almost impossible to see. As with any camouflage, they just have to keep very, very still.

Now, let's see if you can spot the animals hiding in the pages of this book and learn about how they do it. If you have trouble spotting them, turn to pages 88–92.

MAMMALS

AFRICAN LION

The coat of the African lion can vary in colour between buff and brown. It enables the big cat to blend in with its grassland habitat, especially during the dry season when the grass is a similar colour. During the day, it uses this camouflage to hide when stalking prey.

As it creeps slowly towards a target, however, the African lion is generally not alone. Many lions hunt in groups, called prides. Usually, the females in the pride do all the hunting, while the males protect them and their cubs from any dangers, including hyenas and other lions. When hunting, the lionesses try to get as close to their prey as they can without being seen. When the moment is right – perhaps when an antelope looks the other way – they burst from cover and set off on a high speed chase. They are successful in about a third of their hunts.

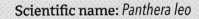

AFRICA

Scientific name: *Panthera leo*

🏠 **Habitat:** African savannahs, grasslands and woodlands south of the Sahara Desert.

🍴 **Diet:** elephants, rhinoceroses, buffalo, giraffes, antelopes, gazelles, zebras, warthogs, porcupines, hyrax, hares and vervet monkeys

🦷 **Predators:** none apart from humans

🌐 **World population:** fewer than 25,000 in the wild

⚠ **Endangered status:** Vulnerable, due to loss of habitat. It is also killed illegally for its fur, claws and teeth, and poisoned by farmers when it attacks cattle. Lions also die from diseases caught from dogs.

MOUNTAIN HARE

The mountain hare switches coat between summer and winter. In summer, its fur is various shades of brown, which blend in with the low-growing tundra, mountain and moorland plants amongst which it hides, although its tail is always white. In winter, it moults into a white or largely white coat to match the snow, but retains black ear tips.

During spring and autumn, the mountain hare might wear its temporary 'in-between' coat when it moults. It matches the patchy snow and vegetation. Hares hide in a form, which is a shallow hollow in the snow or amongst vegetation, and if disturbed they burst out and run in a zigzag fashion. The hare's main enemy is the golden eagle, which has ultra-sharp eyesight to help it spot any movement on the ground. As long as it remains still, the hare is hard to spot and relatively safe.

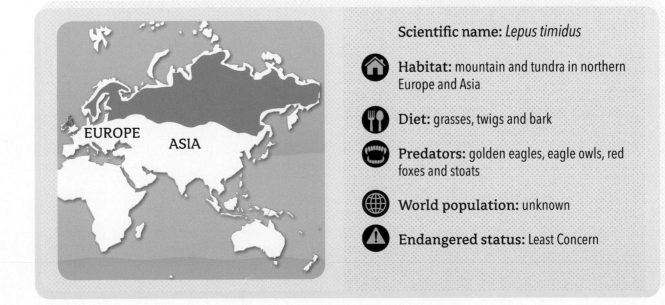

EUROPE

ASIA

Scientific name: *Lepus timidus*

Habitat: mountain and tundra in northern Europe and Asia

Diet: grasses, twigs and bark

Predators: golden eagles, eagle owls, red foxes and stoats

World population: unknown

Endangered status: Least Concern

SNOW LEOPARD

The snow leopard is a secretive mountain cat. Very few people have actually seen one in the wild. The reason is that it is difficult to see. Its pale spotted fur matches the rocky terrain in which it lives, so it can stalk its prey – usually mountain goats and sheep – and pounce at the last moment.

It usually approaches from above and will chase prey down steep mountainsides. The snow leopard has an unusually long and bushy tail that helps it keep its balance as it races across steep cliffs and leaps from one ledge to the next. Its tail can be wrapped around its body and face to help keep it warm when at rest.

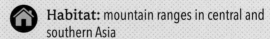

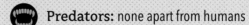
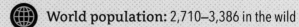

ASIA

Scientific name: *Panthera uncia*

Habitat: mountain ranges in central and southern Asia

Diet: Himalayan blue sheep, Himalayan tahrs, markhor, argalis, marmots, pikas and voles

Predators: none apart from humans

World population: 2,710–3,386 in the wild

Endangered status: Vulnerable, due to destruction of its natural habitat. It is also killed illegally for its fur

BIGHORN SHEEP

Bighorn sheep live high up on the dry, steep, rocky slopes of mountains in North America. They get their name from the large, curved horns on the heads of adult male sheep or rams. They use the horns to smash into an opponent in violent battles at breeding time. The females, or ewes, have smaller headgear.

Large predators in these mountains include mountain lions, bears and wolves. Bighorn lambs are vulnerable to attacks from smaller meat-eaters too – coyotes, bobcats, lynx and golden eagles. The youngsters' defence is twofold: firstly, with great agility they can escape to the narrowest ledges, and secondly, their grey-brown colour is very similar to the rocks on which they stand, so as long as they do not move, they are well camouflaged.

NORTH AMERICA

Scientific name: *Ovis canadensis*

Habitat: mountains in North America, including the Rockies, Sierra Nevada and the deserts of the southwest

Predators: mountain lions, wolves and bears

Diet: grasses and shrubs, but must obtain essential minerals by visiting salt licks

World population: about 67,000 in Canada, USA and Mexico

Endangered status: Least Concern (although the sub-species living in the Sierra Nevada is endangered due to diseases caught from domestic sheep)

SPRINGBOK

The springbok is a long-legged antelope that lives, often in large herds, in the deserts and grasslands of southern Africa. The buff coloured coat on its back helps to conceal it amongst the dry vegetation, especially when it rests. When it is cool, the springbok rests on open ground, but hides amongst bushes when it is hot.

This behaviour also extends to young springbok. Mothers tend to leave their newborn lambs hidden in cover, while they feed. In order to escape the attention of predators, a lamb lies as flat as it can amongst bushes, tall grass or against the desert floor and remains very still. The mother returns from time to time, and after about four weeks they both rejoin the herd. If disturbed, adult springbok leap into the air with stiff legs, behaviour known as 'pronking'. It says to predators 'I'm fit. You can't catch me!'

AFRICA

Scientific name: *Antidorcas marsupialis*

🏠 **Habitat:** deserts, savannah and dry bushlands, shrublands and grasslands of southern Africa

🍴 **Diet:** shrubs and succulents (fleshy plants that retain moisture)

🦷 **Predators:** lions, leopards, cheetahs, caracals, spotted hyenas and wild dogs take adults, and black-backed jackals, southern wild cats, black eagles, martial eagles and tawny eagles target young animals

🌐 **World population:** up to 1,750,000 and increasing

⚠️ **Endangered status:** Least Concern

BROWN-THROATED THREE-TOED SLOTH

Three-toed sloths live high in the canopy of large tropical forest trees. They are not very active, often sleeping for up to 18 hours a day. They can crawl on the ground and even swim, but they spend most of their time in the trees, where they hang upside down. They are almost invisible.

They have greyish-brown to beige-coloured fur, with darker and lighter patches on the face and forehead and could be mistaken for a piece of bark. This disguise is enhanced because the coarse hairs of their coat have microscopic cracks in which live green and red algae, and there is also fungi living amongst them. This 'living' camouflage helps conceal the sloth from its two main enemies – the powerful harpy eagle and the jaguar.

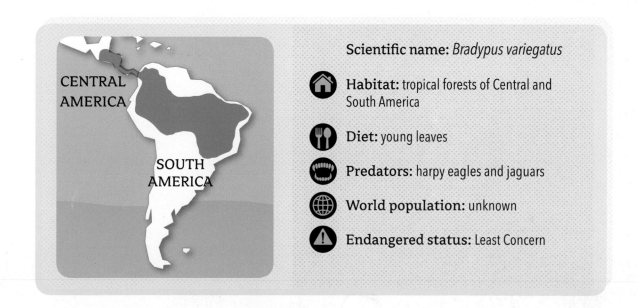

CENTRAL AMERICA

SOUTH AMERICA

Scientific name: *Bradypus variegatus*

🏠 **Habitat:** tropical forests of Central and South America

🍴 **Diet:** young leaves

🦷 **Predators:** harpy eagles and jaguars

🌐 **World population:** unknown

⚠ **Endangered status:** Least Concern

YELLOW-FOOTED ROCK WALLABY

This smaller relative of the kangaroo lives in groups of ten or more on rock faces, cliffs and in gorges in dry mountain ranges, but always close to water. During the heat of the day, it hides away in caves and crevices, coming out in the late afternoon to browse or graze on vegetation close to the foot of rocks and cliffs.

The wallaby's richly coloured fur is similar to the colour of the rocks, so it is well concealed in the rocky landscape. It has few natural predators, the wedge-tailed eagle being the main threat. However, animals introduced to Australia by humans are a real problem. Goats, rabbits and sheep compete with the wallaby for food and cave space and introduced foxes and domestic cats that have gone wild are a threat to wallaby youngsters, known as 'joeys'.

AUSTRALIA

Scientific name: *Petrogale xanthopus*

Habitat: dry, rough terrain and rocky outcrops in Australia

Diet: Wild flowers, herbs, grasses and low trees and shrubs

Predators: wedge-tailed eagle, introduced red foxes and feral cats

World population: less than 10,000

Endangered status: Near Threatened (numbers declined in the 19th and 20th centuries due to hunting for its fur and the species has been slow to recover)

BIRDS

GREAT POTOO

The great potoo is nocturnal. By day, it mimics a branch, usually about 12 m above the ground or maybe higher. It is effectively invisible, but even so, several species of monkey, as well as tayras (a type of weasel) and collared forest falcons take eggs, chicks and fledglings, and even adults if they happen to move.

At night, the potoo becomes a predator itself. It perches on branches closer to the ground and watches for prey, which includes large beetles, crickets and grasshoppers, and it even catches the occasional bat. It grabs the prey, often in midair, and returns to the same branch to eat.

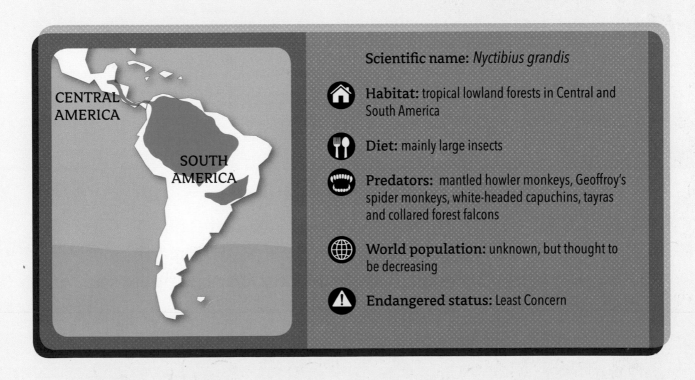

CENTRAL AMERICA

SOUTH AMERICA

Scientific name: *Nyctibius grandis*

Habitat: tropical lowland forests in Central and South America

Diet: mainly large insects

Predators: mantled howler monkeys, Geoffroy's spider monkeys, white-headed capuchins, tayras and collared forest falcons

World population: unknown, but thought to be decreasing

Endangered status: Least Concern

EURASIAN BITTERN

I f it were not for the low-pitched, booming sound the bird makes, it would be hard to know that a bittern was there at all. The colour of its feathers ensures the bird is perfectly camouflaged amongst the reeds.

When disturbed, it points its beak, head and neck vertically, and the long feathers on the throat and breast droop down to hide the neck, so the outline of its body is concealed. It resembles very closely the surrounding reeds. It then freezes. Bird watchers call the behaviour 'bitterning'. Its foghorn-like contact call is heard mainly during the mating season, between January and April, and it is audible on a still night from up to 5 km away.

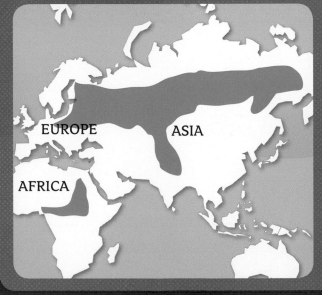

EUROPE

ASIA

AFRICA

Scientific name: *Botaurus stellaris*

Habitat: reed beds in wetlands throughout Europe, Asia and Africa

Diet: fish, small mammals, bird fledglings, amphibians, crustaceans and insects

Predators: red foxes, wild boar and large owls, plus introduced American mink and raccoon dogs

World population: up to 340,000

Endangered status: Least Concern

EGYPTIAN NIGHTJAR

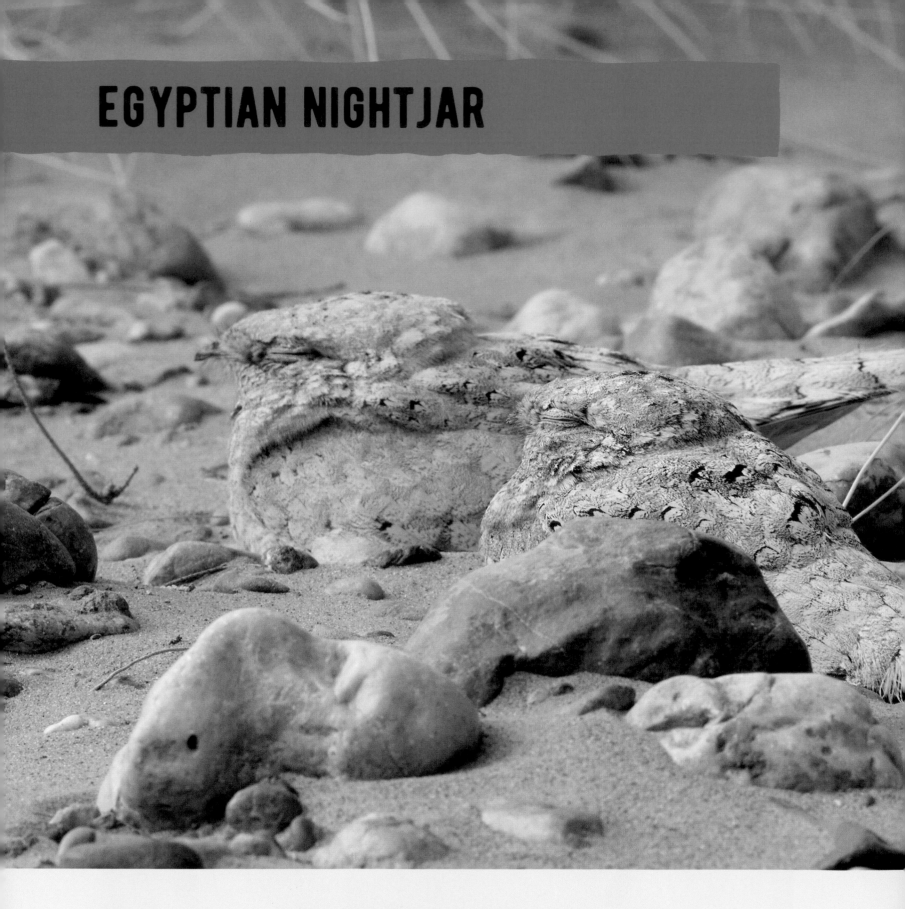

Sand colours, streaked with buff and brown, keep the nightjar from view during the day. Each bird looks a bit different, sitting in places where it can take advantage of its own markings. Like many desert birds, it has no nest.

Its eggs are placed upon the bare ground, where they blend in with the sand and gravel. The eggs are not camouflaged, however, so the mother has to sit on them and rely on her own concealment from predators to protect them. The Egyptian nightjar, like other nightjars, is active at dusk, flying with almost moth-like wing beats, when it catches real moths as it flies.

ASIA

AFRICA

Scientific name: *Caprimulgus aegyptius*

Habitat: desert and dry regions in North Africa and southwest Asia

Diet: moths

Predators: desert foxes and desert cats, owls and hawks

World population: unknown

Endangered status: Least Concern

KAKAPO

The kakapo is a flightless, nocturnal parrot from New Zealand. Its wings are useless, but it has strong legs and can climb trees. During the day, it lurks in the undergrowth rendered invisible by its cryptic (hiding) colouration.

This camouflage was effective against its natural enemies, at a time when birds dominated New Zealand. Flying predators such as the New Zealand falcon and the now-extinct laughing owl, Haast's eagle and Eyles's harrier roamed the skies, and they relied on vision to spot their prey. The introduction of predatory mammals by humans, such as black rats, domestic dogs and cats, red foxes and stoats, which use smell to find a meal, meant that kakapos and their camouflage did not stand a chance. The Maoris also hunted them for their feathers to make ceremonial cloaks, but it was the non-native mammals that eventually brought the species to the edge of extinction.

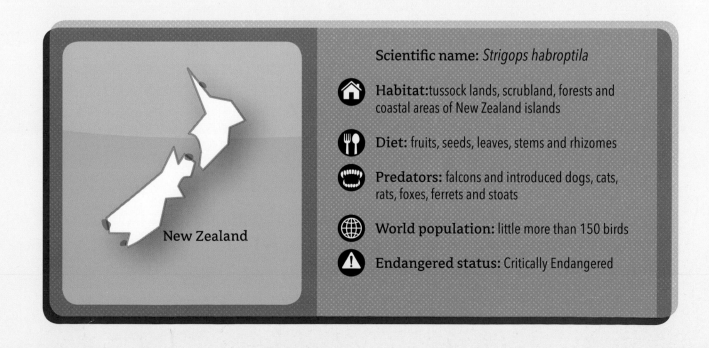

New Zealand

Scientific name: *Strigops habroptila*

Habitat: tussock lands, scrubland, forests and coastal areas of New Zealand islands

Diet: fruits, seeds, leaves, stems and rhizomes

Predators: falcons and introduced dogs, cats, rats, foxes, ferrets and stoats

World population: little more than 150 birds

Endangered status: Critically Endangered

EURASIAN GOLDEN PLOVER

The golden plover's nest is usually a shallow hollow on the ground in flat open areas, such as tundra and highland heaths. It is lined with moss, lichens, leaves and stems. Both sexes incubate their eggs, and the adult birds are well camouflaged in the vegetation.

When the chicks hatch, they leave the nest almost immediately, and, while still guarded by their mother, they must find food for themselves. Their plumage is black-and-yellow above, so they too blend in with the habitat. Remaining still is their main defence. Seen from above they are almost invisible. Even so, they are vulnerable to ground living predators, such as stoats. Adults sometimes pretend to have a broken wing and try to lead an intruder away from their nest or their chicks. Sometimes it works, sometimes it doesn't.

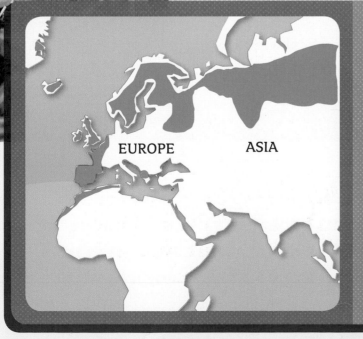

EUROPE   ASIA

Scientific name: *Pluvialis apricaria*

Habitat: breeds on Arctic tundra and northern Eurasian wetlands, grasslands, shrublands, moorlands, heaths and coasts

Diet: crane flies and other flies, beetles, spiders, crustaceans, earthworms, marine worms and snails, with some berries and seeds

Predators: birds of prey, foxes and stoats

World population: up to 1,750,000

Endangered status: Least Concern

EURASIAN EAGLE OWL

One of the largest species of owl is the eagle owl. It is recognised by its distinctive ear tufts. The plumage of its upper parts is tawny (orange-brown) with mottled and streaked dark feathers that match the trees in which it rests during daylight hours, so it is safe from other predators like hawks, eagles and wild cats that hunt by day.

Like many owls, the eagle owl is active mainly at night, when camouflage is ineffective. Instead, it watches and listens for prey from a perch and then swoops down silently to catch it. Its powerful talons kill the prey instantly. Food items can be any small mammals up to the size of a rabbit, and birds as big as a moorhen. Small prey is swallowed whole, while larger items are carried in the talons to a perch and torn apart. The bird has wide-ranging tastes. Over 600 different species have been identified as eagle owl food.

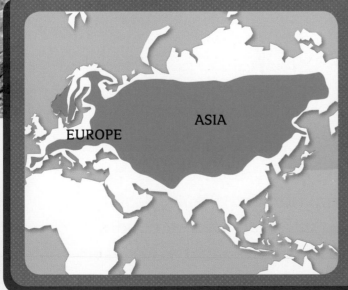

Scientific name: *Bubo bubo*

Habitat: mountains, coniferous forests and steppes

Diet: small mammals and birds, amphibians and reptiles, and fish

Predators: hawks, eagles and wild cats

World population: up to 500,000

Endangered status: Least Concern

ROCK PTARMIGAN

The ptarmigan can be found right across the northern hemisphere, living on the Arctic and sub-arctic tundra, with small, isolated populations on mountains throughout Europe and Asia. It does not migrate great distances, but occupies the same area throughout the year.

Those living on mountains might migrate short distances vertically, heading for higher elevations in summer and the lower slopes in winter. In summer, its mottled plumage blends in with the low-growing vegetation, but in winter it moults into a covering of white feathers, except for a black tail and eye patches. In this way, it matches its snowy surroundings. In the remote places that it lives, it has few natural predators. The golden eagle is its main enemy. The eagle's extraordinary eyesight can spot the movement of a ptarmigan that would be almost invisible to us, so, again, if the ptarmigan remains absolutely still, it will go unnoticed.

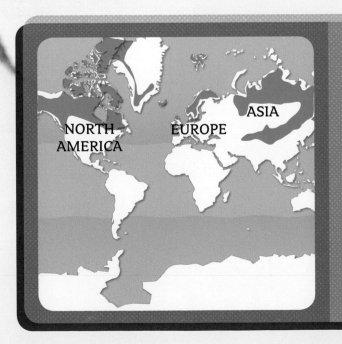

Scientific name: *Lagopus muta*

Habitat: tundra and mountains

Diet: birch and willow buds and catkins, along with berries, seeds, leaves and flowers – chicks eat insects

Predators: red and Arctic foxes, golden eagles, glaucus gulls and skuas

World population: up to 25,000,000, but decreasing due to climate change

Endangered status: Least Concern

REPTILES AND AMPHIBIANS

MOSSY LEAF-TAILED GECKO

The mossy leaf-tailed gecko's large yellow eyes indicate that this lizard is active mainly at night. During the day, it is very difficult to spot. It hides on tree trunks and has special ways in which to disappear from view.

The green and brown camouflage patterns on its skin enable it to blend in with the bark, moss and lichens on the tree. It has flaps of skin on both sides of its body, and on its head, legs and leaf-like tail. These soften its shadow and break up its outline. It can also change colour to help it match its background even more. By remaining very still, it is almost invisible, and therefore safe from daytime predators such as owls and eagles, rats and snakes.

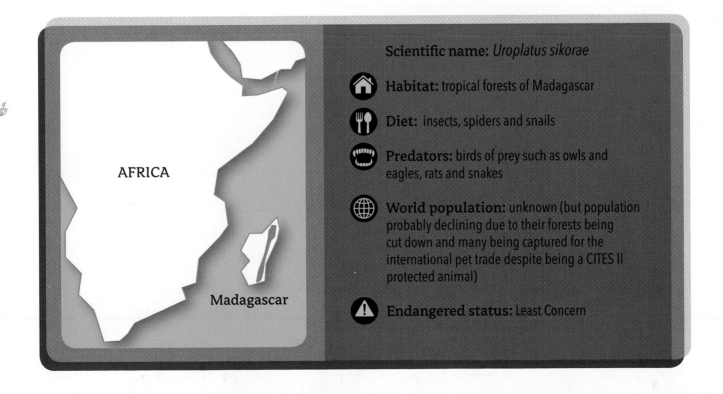

AFRICA

Madagascar

Scientific name: *Uroplatus sikorae*

Habitat: tropical forests of Madagascar

Diet: insects, spiders and snails

Predators: birds of prey such as owls and eagles, rats and snakes

World population: unknown (but population probably declining due to their forests being cut down and many being captured for the international pet trade despite being a CITES II protected animal)

Endangered status: Least Concern

LEAF-NOSED TWIG SNAKE

The large island of Madagascar, off the coast of southern Africa, is also home to the leaf-nosed twig snake. As its common name suggests, the snake resembles a long twig, but males and females have differing disguises at the head end. The male has a long tapering (narrowing) snout, whereas the female has a leaf-shaped snout.

The function of the snout is unknown, but similar shaped structures have been seen on the dangling seedpods of forest plants in Madagascar. They appear to help drain away rainwater. Whatever their function on the snake, they certainly contribute to its camouflage. The twig snake is an ambush predator. It does not move for about 90 per cent of its life, endlessly waiting for something edible to chance by. It hangs from a branch, with its head pointing towards the ground, like a twig, and intercepts lizards. It is venomous and can give a person a painful, but not deadly, bite.

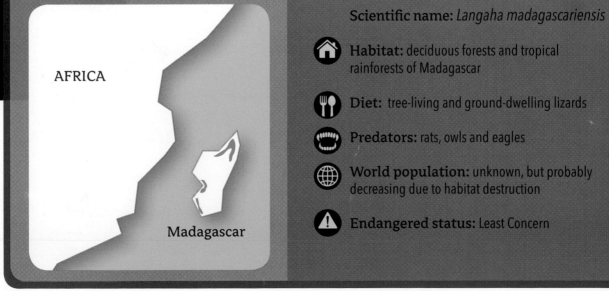

AFRICA

Madagascar

Scientific name: *Langaha madagascariensis*

🏠 **Habitat:** deciduous forests and tropical rainforests of Madagascar

🍴 **Diet:** tree-living and ground-dwelling lizards

🦷 **Predators:** rats, owls and eagles

🌐 **World population:** unknown, but probably decreasing due to habitat destruction

⚠ **Endangered status:** Least Concern

FLAP-NECKED CHAMELEON

The flap-necked chameleon is an inhabitant of the forest, and like many of its relatives, its mottled body colour of various shades of green mean that it is well disguised in its forest home.

Like all chameleons, it is able to change colour, and at first it was thought this is to match its background. Now, we know that the colour change is related more to mood or to cool down or to keep warm. A dark chameleon, for example, will absorb more heat to warm up on a cold morning. The creature also moves in a jerky way, which imitates a leaf blowing in the wind, and it chooses to rest on flimsy branches, where larger predators cannot go. Yet, despite its disguise, it falls prey to snakes, such as the boomslang and twig snake. Snakes rely on detecting the smell of their prey; so all the camouflage in the world will not save the chameleon from them!

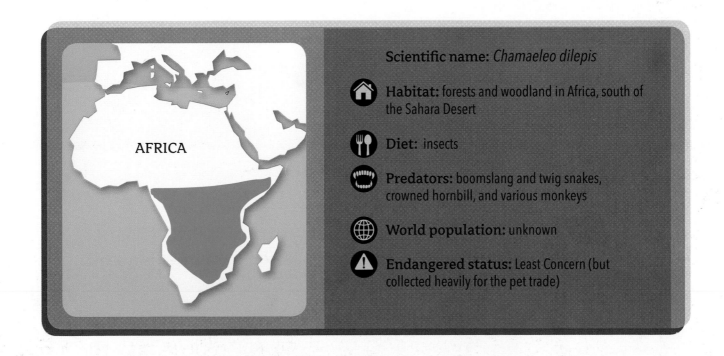

AFRICA

Scientific name: *Chamaeleo dilepis*

Habitat: forests and woodland in Africa, south of the Sahara Desert

Diet: insects

Predators: boomslang and twig snakes, crowned hornbill, and various monkeys

World population: unknown

Endangered status: Least Concern (but collected heavily for the pet trade)

MOSSY FROG

The light and dark green colour of the mossy frog's back matches the moss on stones in its rocky habitat. Numerous bumps and spikes in its skin help the disguise. It has enlarged toe pads that help it clamber about.

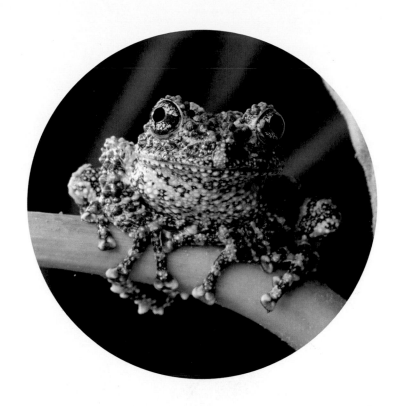

When courting, these frogs can 'throw' their voice, so they are difficult for predators to locate. Females deposit eggs just above the water in rock cavities, so they are safe from egg predators, such as aquatic insect larvae and fish. The tadpoles drop into the water directly below them. While the adult frog's camouflage is effective against many predators, being disguised as a mossy rock is ineffective against snakes. However, the frog has an odd response to an attack: it curls up in a ball and plays dead!

ASIA

Vietnam

Scientific name: *Theloderma corticale*

🏠 **Habitat:** mountain forests, caves and rocky cliffs in northern Vietnam

🍴 **Diet:** insects

🦷 **Predators:** snakes, monkeys, various forest cats and rats

🌐 **World population:** unknown

⚠ **Endangered status:** Least Concern

JAPANESE GIANT SALAMANDER

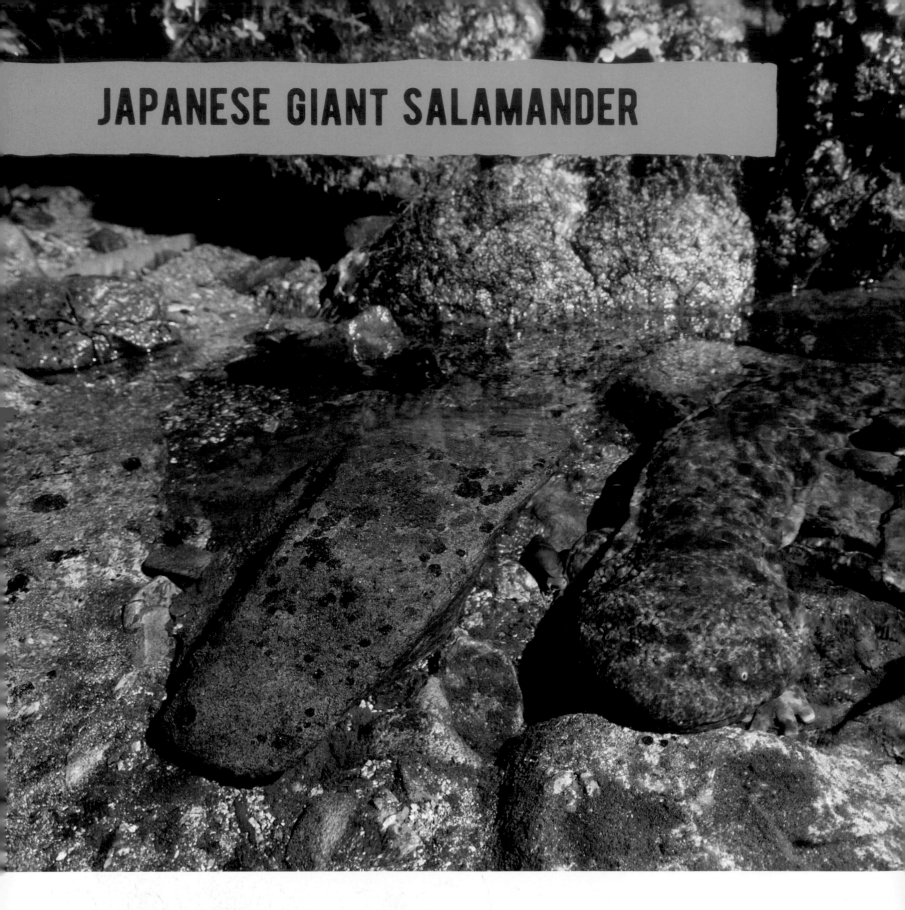

The Japanese giant salamander really is a giant. Adults can be up to 1.5 m long and weigh 25 kg, a far cry from the small salamanders you see in zoos. It lives in rivers with cool, clear, well-oxygenated water on the Japanese islands of Honshu, Shikoku and Kyusyu. Its brown and black mottled skin camouflages it against the mud and stones on the riverbed.

It has very small eyes and poor eyesight, but possesses an enormous mouth that can open as wide as its body. It hunts underwater, detecting the movements and vibrations of its prey with sensory cells that run from its head to its tale. It has few predators in the wild, but if it is disturbed, it releases a milky substance that has the strong smell of Japanese pepper, hence its common Japanese name the 'giant pepper fish'. It can live for over 50 years.

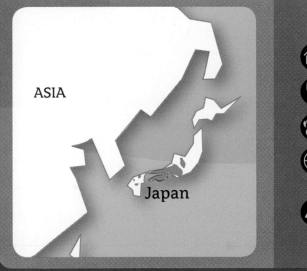

ASIA

Japan

Scientific name: *Andrias japonicus*

Habitat: clear rivers in the forests in Japan

Diet: tree-living and ground-dwelling lizards

Predators: rats, owls and eagles

World population: unknown, but probably decreasing due to habitat destruction

Endangered status: Near Threatened

MALAGASY GROUND BOA

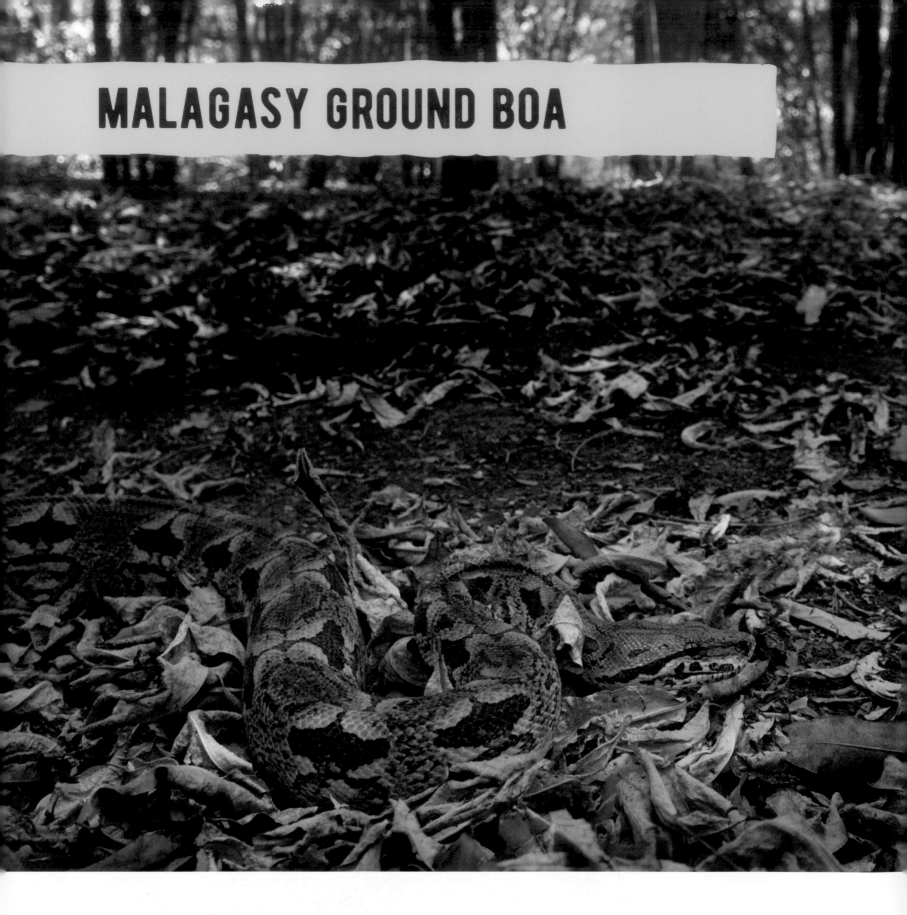

Many of Madagascar's forest animals are camouflaged, and its ground boa is no exception. The snake has a pale reddish-brown colour mixed with grey and a pattern of black or brown elongated diamonds on its body. It also has a series of black oval markings and red blotches bordered in white along its side.

These markings help it to blend in with both the leaf litter on the forest floor and amongst the leaves and branches in the trees. They also help to blur the animal's outline when it moves, so it is even invisible even when close to its prey. The boa grows to more than 3 m long, making it the largest of the island's snakes. It feeds on lemurs, monkey-like primates that are unique to Madagascar. Heat-sensitive pits in its face detect the heat from its victim's body. It then grabs it in its mouth, throws coils around the lemur's body, and squeezes until the heart stops beating. Then it swallows the lemur whole.

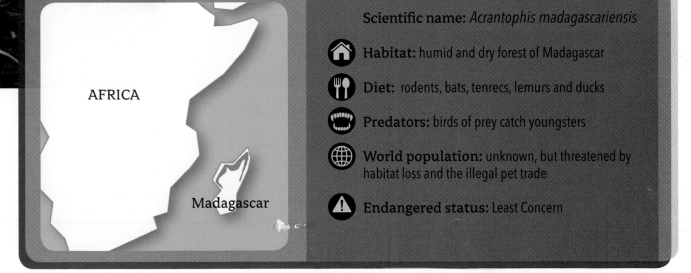

AFRICA

Madagascar

Scientific name: *Acrantophis madagascariensis*

Habitat: humid and dry forest of Madagascar

Diet: rodents, bats, tenrecs, lemurs and ducks

Predators: birds of prey catch youngsters

World population: unknown, but threatened by habitat loss and the illegal pet trade

Endangered status: Least Concern

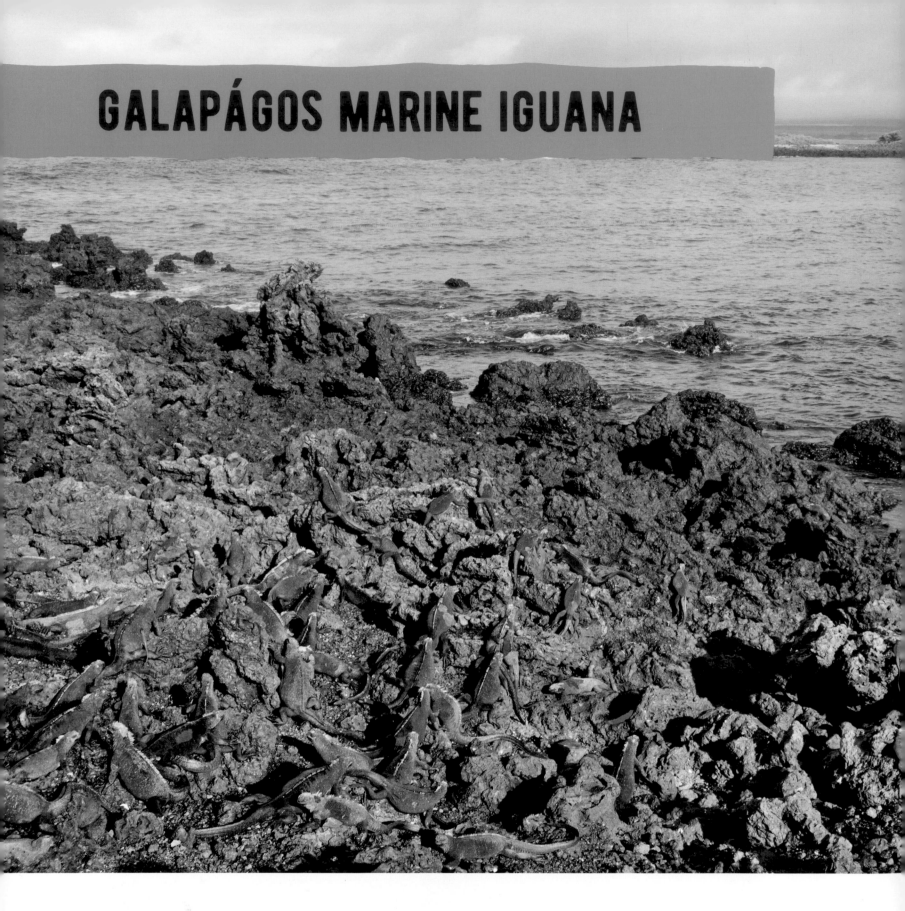

GALAPÁGOS MARINE IGUANA

The world's only species of marine lizard lives on the rocky shore of the Galapágos Islands. Body colour varies between islands. Those living on black volcanic rocks tend to be dark.

The colour gives them some degree of camouflage, and because darker colours absorb more light and therefore more heat from the sun, it also enables them to warm up quickly when they leave the water. The reptiles generally stay close to the water's edge, but females can be found digging nests up to 2 km inland. Away from their rocky background and the sea, they are vulnerable to attacks by Galapágos hawks and Galapágos racer snakes. The iguanas, however, have an early warning system. When hawks fly over, the local mockingbirds cry in alarm, and the iguanas dive into the sea.

CENTRAL
AMERICA

Galapágos
Islands

SOUTH
AMERICA

Scientific name: *Amblyrhynchus cristatus*

🏠 **Habitat:** rocky seashore in Galapágos Islands

🍴 **Diet:** marine red and green algae (seaweeds)

🦷 **Predators:** Galapágos hawks and racer snakes

🌐 **World population:** up to 150,000

⚠ **Endangered status:** Vulnerable

CROCODILEFISH

Along body, up to 50 cm long, and a flattened snout, like a duck's bill or crocodile's snout, prompted marine biologists to call this fish a 'crocodilefish'.

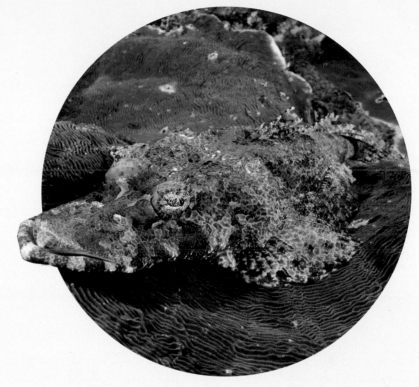

It is coloured to resemble coral sand and has root-shaped eye lappets, which are little flaps of skin that help to break up the black iris of its globular eyes and improve its camouflage. The crocodilefish is an ambush predator. It lies buried in the sand, with only its eyes showing. When a fish approaches and reaches a critical distance in front of its snout, the crocodilefish erupts from the seabed. It strikes at lightning speed and engulfs its prey in its large mouth.

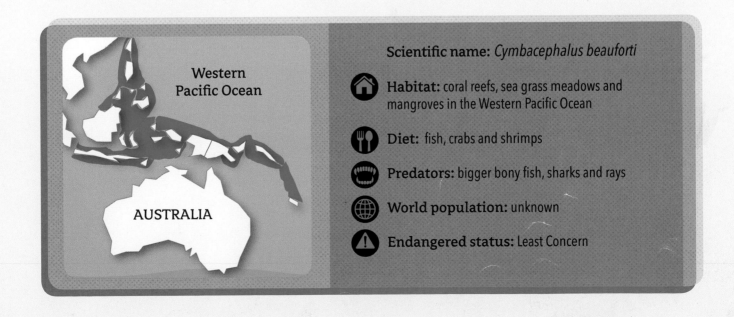

Western Pacific Ocean

AUSTRALIA

Scientific name: *Cymbacephalus beauforti*

Habitat: coral reefs, sea grass meadows and mangroves in the Western Pacific Ocean

Diet: fish, crabs and shrimps

Predators: bigger bony fish, sharks and rays

World population: unknown

Endangered status: Least Concern

PYGMY SEAHORSE

Of the six known species of pygmy seahorse, this was the first to be recognised. It lives exclusively on fan corals, and closely matches their colour and appearance. It is so well camouflaged scientists only discovered it existed when they took a coral into the laboratory.

The tiny fish, no bigger than 2.7 cm long, has a grasping tail with which it anchors itself to its coral, and it never leaves it for its entire life. It is a stealth predator, and it has to be. The prey is exceedingly small, usually tiny copepods, but these are hard to catch. They can jet out of danger, moving at 500 body-lengths per second (compared to a cheetah running at 30 body lengths per second at full tilt). The seahorse has to get within a millimetre before striking. It then sucks in its prey through its tube-shaped jaws before the copepod can escape.

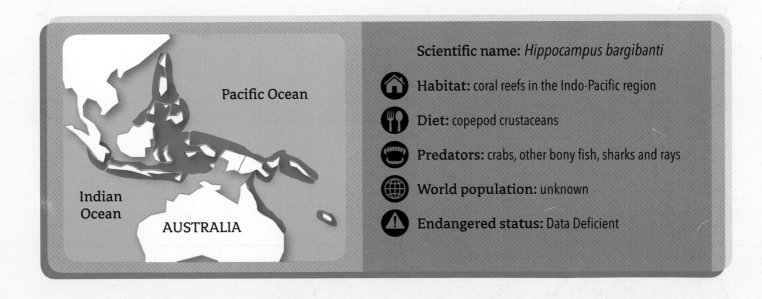

Pacific Ocean

Indian Ocean

AUSTRALIA

Scientific name: *Hippocampus bargibanti*

Habitat: coral reefs in the Indo-Pacific region

Diet: copepod crustaceans

Predators: crabs, other bony fish, sharks and rays

World population: unknown

Endangered status: Data Deficient

SARGASSUM FISH

This little fish lives in the Sargasso Sea, part of the tropical Atlantic, and along coasts elsewhere in the world. It is usually found amongst floating sargassum seaweed, within which it is well camouflaged as its body and fins are decorated with weed-like projections.

The Sargassum fish's flexible pectoral fins enable it to clamber about in the seaweed where it is a voracious ambush predator. The first spine of its dorsal fin is modified as a fishing lure. It attracts small fishes and shrimps, which also take refuge amongst the floating seaweed. When prey come close enough, in a fraction of a second, the sargassum fish darts forward, expels water through its gills, expands its mouth to many times its original size, and sucks in its prey. If it is threatened itself, it can leap onto the top of the seaweed and escape any underwater predator, such as sharks and swordfish.

Sargasso Sea

Scientific name: *Histrio histrio*

🏠 **Habitat:** open ocean and coastal regions wherever floating mats of Sargassum seaweed grow

🍴 **Diet:** small fish and crustaceans

🦷 **Predators:** larger bony fish, such as swordfish, and several species of shark

🌐 **World population:** unknown

⚠ **Endangered status:** Least Concern

LEOPARD FLOUNDER

Flatfish look as if they are resting on their belly, but actually, they are lying on their side, with both eyes on the same side of their body. The leopard flounder is a left-eye flounder, because its right eye has evolved to be on the left side of its body with the left eye.

The colour of its skin on that side, with spots, blotches and ring-like markings, matches the sandy or muddy seabed on which it rests, so it is well camouflaged. It can also become light or dark quite rapidly depending on its background. In this way, it is invisible to larger predators, such as sharks and dolphins. If it should swim towards the surface, it is said to lose all colour and appear almost transparent.

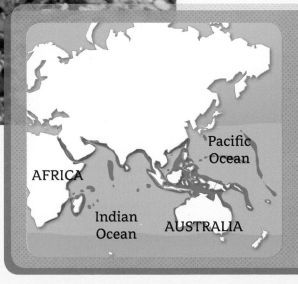

AFRICA

Pacific
Ocean

Indian
Ocean

AUSTRALIA

Scientific name: *Bothus pantherinus*

Habitat: coral reef flats in the Pacific and Indian oceans

Diet: worms, clams, crabs, lobsters, sponges and other tiny organisms that live on the seabed

Predators: larger bony fish, sharks and rays

World population: unknown

Endangered status: Least Concern

TASSELLED WOBBEGONG SHARK

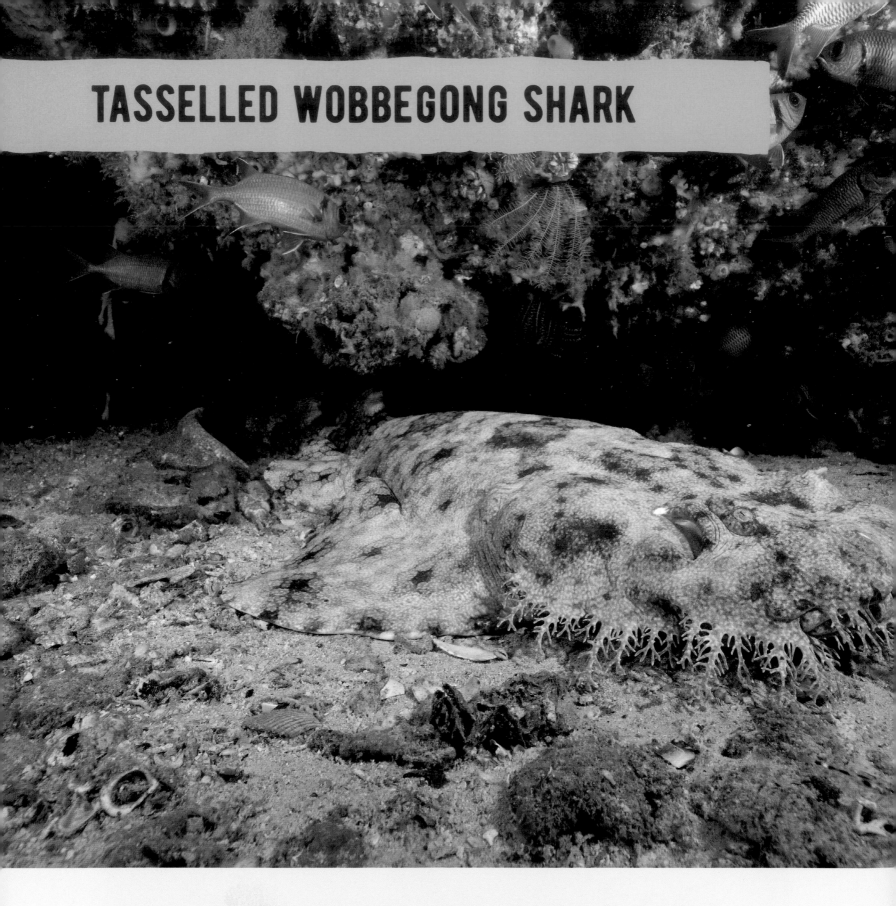

This 1.25-m-long member of the carpet shark family looks like coral. Its body is flattened, and its head and chin are festooned with a fringe of skin flaps. It has a complex colour pattern of spots and blotches that camouflage the shark.

During the day, it is almost impossible to see, so it is in a good position to ambush passing fish and crustaceans. It lies motionless, except that it will wave its tail slowly and provocatively, mimicking a small fish. It even has a spot on its tail, which looks like a fish's eye, to lure in other predators. If one comes too close, the shark grabs it. At night, it emerges from its daytime resting place and actively pursues prey, such as nocturnal squirrelfish and soldierfish.

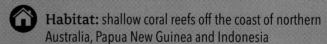

Scientific name: *Eucrossorhinus dasypogon*

Habitat: shallow coral reefs off the coast of northern Australia, Papua New Guinea and Indonesia

Diet: small fish and crustaceans

Predators: larger bony fish, sharks and rays

World population: unknown

Endangered status: Least Concern

LEAFY SEADRAGON

With many lobes of skin resembling kelp fronds, this species in the seahorse and pipefish family is extremely well camouflaged as seaweed. It also rocks back and forth, mimicking the movement of seaweed in the waves.

It is a slow mover, propelled along by tiny, almost transparent, fins on its neck and near its tail. Leafy seadragons do not travel far, maybe a few hundred metres, but always return to the same spot, where they can remain almost stationary for two or three days before setting out again. They rely totally on camouflage to hide from predators, such as larger fish, and, as they do not have a prehensile tail like seahorses, they sometimes get washed ashore during storms. Like seahorses, however, male rather than female seadragons look after the eggs.

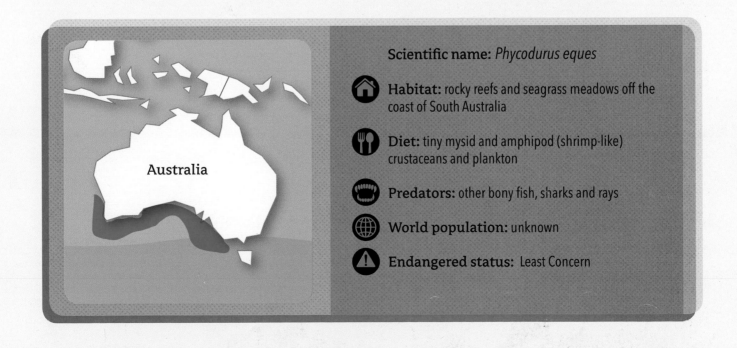

Australia

Scientific name: *Phycodurus eques*

🏠 **Habitat:** rocky reefs and seagrass meadows off the coast of South Australia

🍴 **Diet:** tiny mysid and amphipod (shrimp-like) crustaceans and plankton

🦷 **Predators:** other bony fish, sharks and rays

🌐 **World population:** unknown

⚠️ **Endangered status:** Least Concern

REEF STONEFISH

The stonefish lives amongst corals, coral rubble and rocks. The pattern on its body gives it the appearance of a coral or rock covered with seaweed. It is a 'sit-and-wait' predator, which gulps in any small marine creature passing close to its mouth.

Seaweed and tiny sea creatures grow on its body, which not only help the disguise, but also attract small fish and shrimps to the stonefish's mouth. Its camouflage also helps hide it from larger predators, such as tiger sharks, which sometimes eat stonefish. The stonefish, however, has another defence. It is the world's most venomous fish. On its back are 13 sharp, stiff hollow spines with venom sacs attached. It is difficult to spot, so a human could easily stand on the fish. Its spines have been known to pierce a leather boot, and they deliver venom that can kill a person. Tiger sharks however appear to be immune.

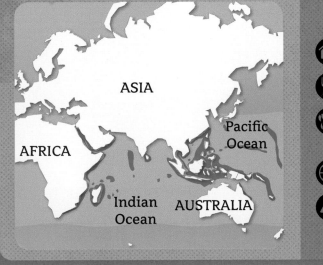

Scientific name: *Synanceia verrucosa*

🏠 **Habitat:** tropical coral reefs in the Pacific and Indian oceans

🍴 **Diet:** small fish, shrimps and other marine crustaceans

🦷 **Predators:** larger bony fish, such as groupers, and sharks, such as tiger sharks

🌐 **World population:** unknown

⚠️ **Endangered status:** Least Concern

INSECTS AND SPIDERS

BRIMSTONE BUTTERFLY

For many people, the brimstone butterfly is the first sign of spring. On warm days, they emerge from hibernation amongst piles of twigs or grass tussocks as early as January. Both caterpillars and adults rely on camouflage to reduce the risk of predation, mainly from birds and wasps.

Caterpillars are green, and, if disturbed, lie motionless in the midribs of leaves, where they are well disguised. Adults mimic the leaves themselves. Individuals lucky enough to survive may live for a long time, up to 12 months, making it one of the longest living butterflies, although, of course, for a large part of that time, the butterfly is in hibernation.

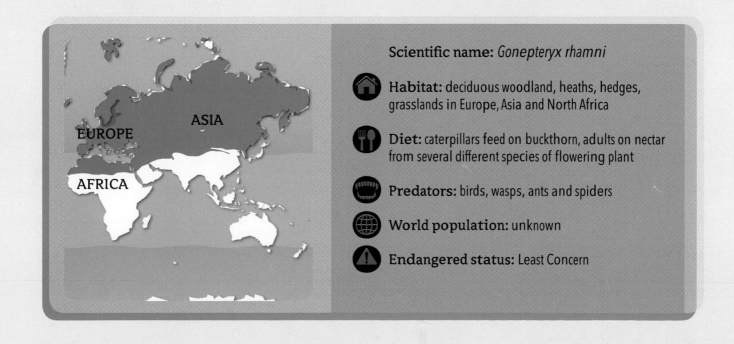

Scientific name: *Gonepteryx rhamni*

Habitat: deciduous woodland, heaths, hedges, grasslands in Europe, Asia and North Africa

Diet: caterpillars feed on buckthorn, adults on nectar from several different species of flowering plant

Predators: birds, wasps, ants and spiders

World population: unknown

Endangered status: Least Concern

STONE GRASSHOPPER

These grasshoppers live in hot dry, rocky places, such as the Brandberg Mountains in Namibia, where not only the patterns on their body help camouflage them amongst the granite rocks, but also their behaviour.

In order to disappear from view, the grasshopper must be aware of its background so it can choose to be standing in the right place. It must also stand with its body pointing in the right direction, so it is aligned with the direction of the grain in the rocks. And, for its disguise to be totally effective, it has to remain as still as a rock. We know the stone grasshopper is a 'grasshopper' because it has a pair of short antennae, and is therefore sometimes known as a 'short-horned grasshopper' (crickets and bush crickets are long-horned).

AFRICA

Scientific name: species in the family Pamphagidae

Habitat: rocky mountain areas in deserts in southern Africa

Diet: grasses

Predators: eggs eaten by bee flies, ground beetles and blister beetles; young caught by ants, robber flies and wasps; adults taken by birds, reptiles and small mammals

World population: unknown

Endangered status: Not Evaluated

TREE TRUNK SPIDER

These spiders are recognised by the two unusually long silk spinnerets (the organs that make the spider's web) that are almost as long as their abdomens. It gave rise to the nickname 'two-tailed spiders'. They are extremely well camouflaged and resemble the dark, rough surface of bark.

Their camouflage helps protect them from predators, such as birds, and like most other spiders, they are predators themselves. This species, however, catches its prey in an unusual way. The spider spins a light coating of threads over the bark and waits for an insect to stray into it. It then directs its large spinnerets at the trapped victim and circles it, covering it in a silky net. The spider pierces the net and injects venom, which digests the prey. The spider then sucks up the nutritious broth.

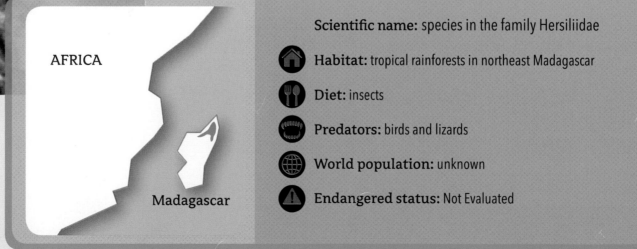

AFRICA

Madagascar

Scientific name: species in the family Hersiliidae

🏠 **Habitat:** tropical rainforests in northeast Madagascar

🍴 **Diet:** insects

Predators: birds and lizards

🌐 **World population:** unknown

⚠️ **Endangered status:** Not Evaluated

TROPICAL KATYDID

Katydids or bush crickets are 'long-horned grasshoppers', which means they have long, wispy antennae (unlike other grasshoppers and locusts that have short antennae). They are mainly tree-living insects that are active at night, and many species are camouflaged to match the habitat in which they live.

The katydid in the picture is mimicking mosses and lichens growing on a tree trunk. During the day, the insect adopts a special roosting posture that locks it in place, so predators might think it is either dead or simply part of the vegetation. If a predator, such as a bird, should take an interest, some katydids have large, brightly coloured eyespots on the undersides of their wings. When attacked they flash these at the attacker, so the insect looks a lot bigger than it really is. Others make a sudden, startling sound.

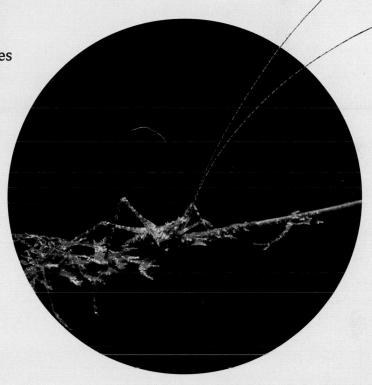

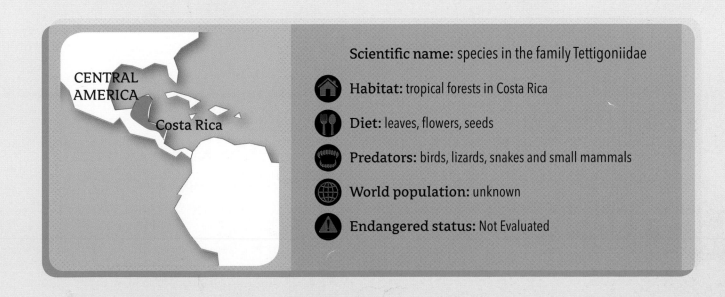

CENTRAL
AMERICA

Costa Rica

Scientific name: species in the family Tettigoniidae

Habitat: tropical forests in Costa Rica

Diet: leaves, flowers, seeds

Predators: birds, lizards, snakes and small mammals

World population: unknown

Endangered status: Not Evaluated

GOLDENROD CRAB SPIDER

In North America, the goldenrod spider gets its name from the way it frequents goldenrod flowers in the autumn, but it is not restricted to them. The spiders can be yellow or white depending on the colour of the flower they occupy, and they can change colour at will.

When occupying a yellow flower, the spider changes colour by secreting a liquid yellow pigment into the outer cells of its body. It takes 10-25 days to complete the transformation. If the spider hunts in a white flower, the yellow pigment is moved to lower layers in the body, so that glands filled with a white substance are visible. This takes about six days. If the spider remains in a white flower for too long, the yellow pigment is got rid of. This means that when it goes to a yellow flower again, it has to manufacture the yellow pigment first, before it can begin to change colour, so it all takes much longer.

NORTH AMERICA

EUROPE

Scientific name: *Misumena vatia*

Habitat: flowers in meadows and prairies in North America and throughout Europe

Diet: insects

Predators: shrews, birds, lizards, larger spiders, ants and wasps

World population: unknown

Endangered status: Not Evaluated

LAPPET MOTH

The lappet moth, like many moths, is active at night, especially during June and July, when it can be attracted to artificial lights. It also flies sometimes during the day. At rest, it resembles a cluster of dried oak leaves, so it can hide amongst the leaf litter on the woodland floor.

The lappet moth has an obvious 'snout', and its hind wings stick out in front of the forewings when stationary. Females are bigger than males, and they attract the opposite sex with a scent that smells like burned wood or charcoal. Caterpillars hatch out in late summer, and become dormant when the weather becomes cold. They hibernate for the winter on stems near the base of the food plant. The moth gets its name from the 'lappets' or fleshy skirts along the sides of the caterpillar, which break up its outline when motionless on a twig.

Scientific name: *Gastropacha quercifolia*

Habitat: deciduous woodland and hedgerows in Europe and Asia

Diet: caterpillars feed on hawthorn, blackthorn, crab apple, willow and oak, but the adults do not feed

Predators: birds, ants and wasps

World population: unknown, but naturalists have noticed a decline in recent years

Endangered status: Not Evaluated

MOSS MIMIC STICK INSECT

Stick insects are known for the way they mimic twigs, but the moss mimic stick insect takes it to an extreme. Its body and legs have mossy and lichen-like appendages that enable it to almost disappear into its daytime resting place on moss-covered twigs.

When it moves, it does so by swaying back and forth as if waving in a gentle breeze. This hesitant walk is similar to the way the plants move in the wind and enhances the camouflage effect. This species is active mainly at night, when it feeds on the leaves of orchid plants that grow on the trees. Enemies include spiders and birds, but only if they can spot the insect. Some species of stick insect have spikes or foul-smelling liquid to defend themselves with if attacked, and they can re-grow lost limbs. Whether this species has these defences is unknown.

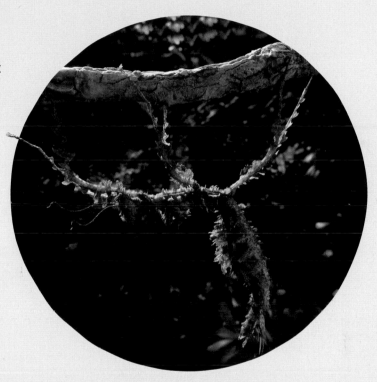

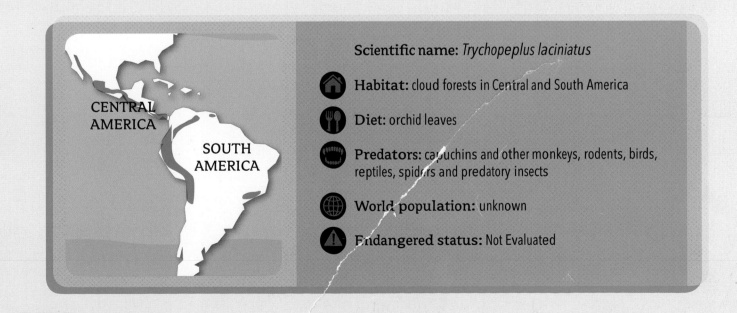

CENTRAL AMERICA

SOUTH AMERICA

Scientific name: *Trychopeplus laciniatus*

🏠 **Habitat:** cloud forests in Central and South America

🍴 **Diet:** orchid leaves

🦷 **Predators:** capuchins and other monkeys, rodents, birds, reptiles, spiders and predatory insects

🌐 **World population:** unknown

⚠️ **Endangered status:** Not Evaluated

ANIMALS REVEALED

MAMMALS

PAGE 10 African lion

PAGE 12 Mountain hare

PAGE 16 Bighorn sheep

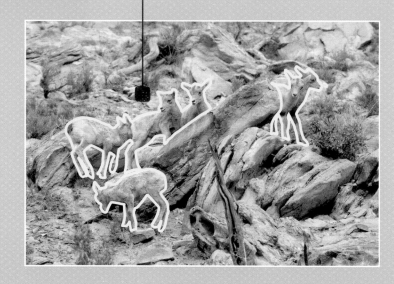

PAGE 14
Snow leopard

PAGE 20 Brown-throated three-toed sloth

PAGE 22 Yellow-footed rock wallaby

PAGE 18 Springbok

BIRDS

PAGE 26 Great potoo

PAGE 28 Eurasian bittern

PAGE 30 Egyptian nightjar

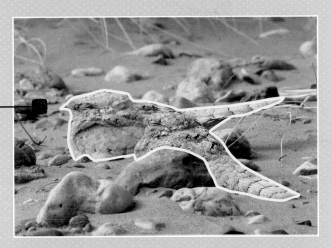

PAGE 32 Kakapo

PAGE 34 Eurasian golden plover

PAGE 36 Eurasian eagle owl

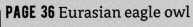

PAGE 38 Rock ptarmigan

REPTILES AND AMPHIBIANS

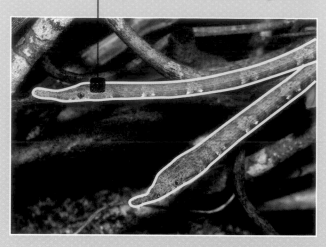

PAGE 44 Leaf-nosed twig snake

PAGE 42
Mossy
leaf-tailed
gekko

PAGE 48
Mossy frog

PAGE 46
Flap-necked
chameleon

PAGE 50
Japanese giant
salamander

PAGE 52
Malagasy ground boa

PAGE 54 Galapagos marine iguana

FISH

PAGE 60 Pygmy seahorse

PAGE 58
Crocodilefish

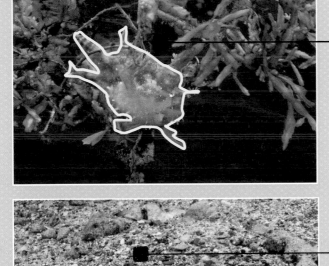

PAGE 62
Sargassum
fish

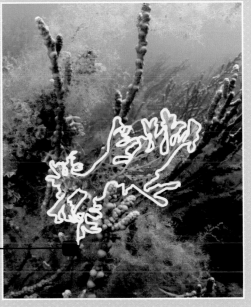

PAGE 64
Leopard flounder

PAGE 68
Leafy seadragon

PAGE 70 Reef stonefish

PAGE 66 Tassled wobbegong shark

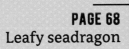

INSECTS AND SPIDERS

PAGE 74
Brimstone
butterfly

PAGE 76 Stone grasshopper

PAGE 78
Tree trunk
spider

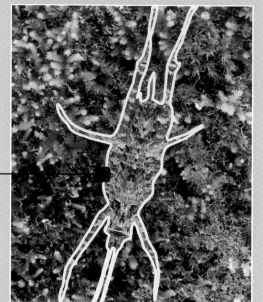

PAGE 80
Tropical
katydid

PAGE 82
Goldenrod crab
spider

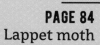

PAGE 84
Lappet moth

PAGE 86 Moss mimic stick insect

GLOSSARY

abdomen the rear segment of an insect or spider

adapt to change, or to change something, to suit different conditions

adaptation the process in which a living thing changes slightly over time to be able to continue to exist in a particular environment

algae plant-like organisms that can make their own food using energy from the sun

ambush to catch something using surprise

antenna long, thin sensory organs that are found on the heads of insects and crustaceans

aquatic living or growing in water

buff a pale, yellowish-brown colour

copepod a tiny crustacean that lives in the sea or in lakes

coral a hard substance formed in the sea from masses of shells of very small sea animals, usually orange or red in color

CITES II abbreviation for Convention on International Trade in Endangered Species,

a treaty to protect endangered plants and animals

crustacean a type of animal that lives in water and has a hard outer shell

deciduous refers to trees that lose their leaves in winter

dormant not active

elevation the height of a place above the level of the sea

fledgling a young bird that has grown feathers and is learning to fly

frond a long, thin leaf of a plant

fungi plant-like organisms that break down dead material in order to obtain food

grassland a large area of land covered with grass

hibernation the state of being asleep for the winter

inanimate not alive

ineffective not working very well

introduce to bring a plant, animal or disease to a place for the first time

kelp a large, brown plant that grows in the sea

lichen a grey, green or yellow plant-like organism that grows on rocks, walls and trees

lure something made to look like prey to attract a predator

Maoris native people who live in New Zealand

marine related to the sea

migrate to travel to another part of the world where conditions are better

mimic to copy

moorland an upland area with low growing plants

mottled blotchy, with spots or patches of colour

moult to get rid of skin, fur or feathers in order to grow new

nocturnal active at night

oxygenated containing a lot of oxygen

pectoral the front fins on a fish

pigment the natural colouring of animal and plant tissues

pitch the degree of highness or lowness of a sound

plumage a bird's feathers

prehensile able to hold on to things, especially by curling around them

primate group of animals including apes, monkeys and lemurs

projection bit that sticks out

rhizome a stem of some plants that grows horizontally along or under the ground and produces roots and leaves

salt lick a place where animals go to lick salt from the ground

savannah a large, flat area of land covered with grass, usually with few trees, that is found in hot countries, especially in Africa

sensory connected with the physical senses of touch, smell, taste, hearing and sight

species a group of living things that have similar characteristics

stalk to creep up slowly and unseen on prey

steppe a large area of land with grass but no trees, especially in eastern Europe, Russia, and Central Asia

tundra area of low-growing plants, no trees and frozen soil, where the climate is very cold

tussock a small area of grass that is thicker or longer than the grass growing around it

vegetation plants

FURTHER INFORMATION

BOOKS

Find out all about some of the world's most rare and endangered creatures from the IUCN Red List of Threatened Species in:
Endangered Wildlife series by Anita Ganeri, Wayland, 2020

An illustrated introduction to animal camouflage:
Look Again: Secrets of Animal Camouflage by Steve Jenkins, Houghton Mifflin Harcourt, 2019

Discover the animals with the most sophisticated and highly-developed survival techniques and how the process of evolution has helped perfect them: in
Nature's Best: Display and Camouflage by Tom Jackson, Wayland, 2018

Uncover Earth's iconic landmarks and habitats, and the plants and animals that live there in:
Wildlife Worlds series by Tim Harris, Franklin Watts, 2019

WEBSITES

Find out about more animals in disguise:
www.pitara.com/science-for-kids/5ws-and-h/how-do-animals-camouflage

Look up whether animals or plants are in danger on the IUCN Red List website:
www.iucnredlist.org

Lots of fascinating facts about animals. The site covers mammals, reptiles, amphibians, fish and birds:
www.nationalgeographic.com/animals/index/

IUCN RED LIST

IUCN stands for the International Union for the Conservation of Nature. It has compiled a 'Red List' of plants and animals that indicates whether a species is in danger of extinction or not. It is updated regularly. The categories used are as follows:

Extinct: beyond reasonable doubt that the species does not exist anymore

Extinct in the wild: survives only in captivity

Critically Endangered: in serious danger of going extinct

Endangered: high risk of extinction

Vulnerable: without people's help, heading for extinction

Near Threatened: high risk of being extinct in the future

Least Concern: unlikely to be extinct in the future

Data Deficient: little information available to assess the species' future

Not Evaluated: very little, if any, information available

INDEX